THE NATURE COMPANY · YOUNG DISCOVERIES LIBRARY

Scaly Things

Written by Klay Lamprell

TIME
LIFE
BOOKS

The Nature Company Young Discoveries Library is published by Time-Life Books.

Conceived and produced by
Weldon Owen Pty Limited
43 Victoria Street, McMahons Point,
NSW, 2060, Australia
A member of the
Weldon Owen Group of Companies
Sydney • San Francisco

THE NATURE COMPANY
Priscilla Wrubel, Ed Strobin, Steve Manning,
Georganne Papac, Tracy Fortini

TIME-LIFE BOOKS
Time-Life Books is a division of Time Life Inc.
Time-Life is a trademark of Time Warner Inc. U.S.A.

Vice President and Publisher: Terry Newell
Editorial Director: Donia A. Steele
Director of New Product Development: Regina Hall
Director of Sales: Neil Levin
Director of Financial Operations: J. Brian Birky

WELDON OWEN Pty Limited
President: John Owen
Publisher: Sheena Coupe
Managing Editor: Rosemary McDonald
Project Editor: Helen Bateman
Text Editor: Claire Craig
Art Director: Sue Burk
Designer: Robyn Latimer
Picture Research: Libby Frederico
Production Manager: Caroline Webber
Vice President, International Sales: Stuart Laurence
Coeditions Director: Derek Barton
Subject Consultants: Dr. David Kirshner,
Dr. George McKay, Craig Sowden

Library of Congress
Cataloging-in-Publication Data
Scaly things / Klay Lamprell.
    p. cm. -- (Young discoveries)

   ISBN 0-7835-4842-7

   1. Scales (Reptiles)--Juvenile literature.
2. Body covering (Anatomy)--Juvenile literature.
[1. Scales (Reptiles) 2. Body covering (Anatomy)]
I. Title. II. Series.
QL942.L35   1996
597.9--dc20   96-12346

Manufactured by Mandarin Offset
Printed in China

A Weldon Owen Production

Contents

Looking at Scaly Things

Scales are hard pieces of skin, like fingernails, which cover the bodies of many creatures. Most scaly creatures, such as fish, snakes, lizards, turtles and crocodiles, are cold-blooded animals. Mammals are warm-blooded. Some, such as mice and opossums, have scaly tails. Only one mammal, the pangolin, has scales on its body. The shape and size of a creature's scales give clues to where it lives, what it eats and what it is eaten by.

▲ The scales on a fish are loosely attached, and can come off.

Which scaly creatures here are cold-blooded?

4

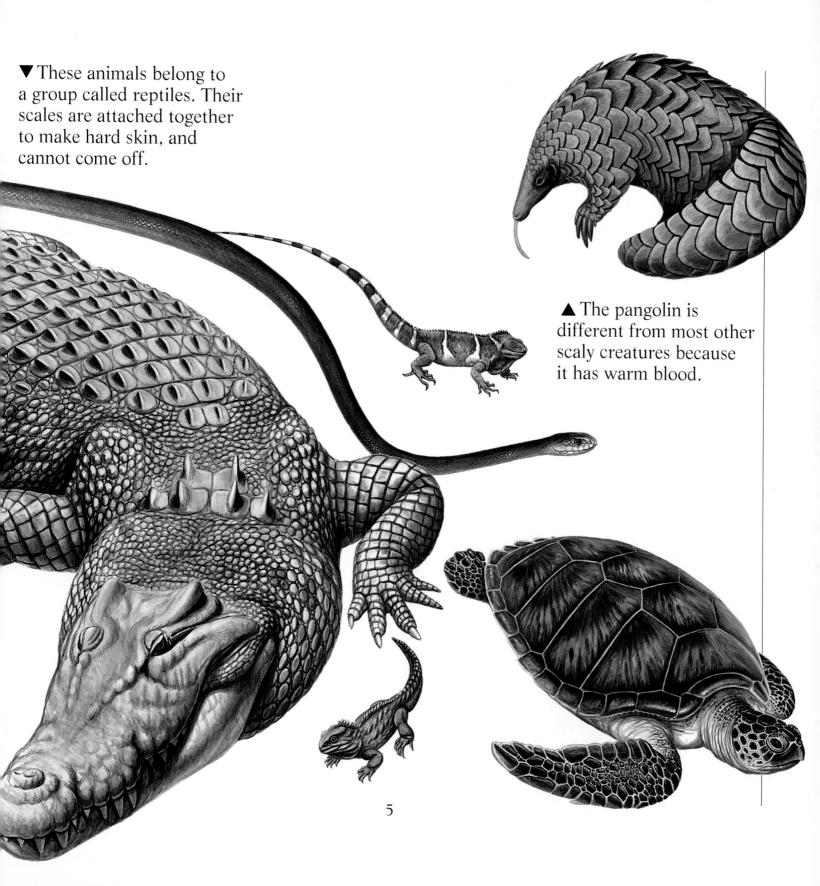

▼These animals belong to a group called reptiles. Their scales are attached together to make hard skin, and cannot come off.

▲The pangolin is different from most other scaly creatures because it has warm blood.

5

Slow and Steady

What shapes can you see in this tortoise's shell?

Turtles have scales on all parts of their bodies, even on their bony shells. Turtles that live on land, called tortoises, mostly have shells that are high and round. They can pull their head and tail inside the shell to hide from enemies. The shells are very heavy, which is one reason tortoises move so slowly. They eat things that also move slowly, like snails, or things that do not move at all, like plants. Some turtles can stay alive for months without food.

◀ The Galápagos Islands tortoise is enormous compared to the South American red-footed tortoise and the tiny spider tortoise.

6

▶ This tortoise shell is empty. Tortoises cannot crawl out of their shells, which are their skeletons.

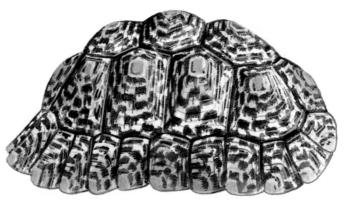

▼ Tortoise legs have claws for walking and digging.

◀ This radiated tortoise, from the island of Madagascar, could live to be more than 100 years old.

A chameleon's tongu

Chameleons

Chameleon feet grip, like hands, onto branches.

A chameleon hides from its predators by changing the color of its body. In the day, it matches the plants and rocks around it. At night, it turns pale and stays very still, like a leaf on a twig. Chameleons can make one eye look one way while the other is looking another way. This helps them to spot predators coming from different directions. It also helps them find insects to eat.

14

as long as its body

▼ Male Knysna dwarf
chameleons warn off other
males by changing from
all-green into bright
patterns of different colors.

▲ This chameleon
extends its long, very
sticky tongue to catch
food in the next tree.

◀ A basilisk lizard has scaly fringes on the toes of its back feet that allow it to run on water.

Lizards with Frills

When threatened, the Australian frilled lizard can run on its two back legs.

Lizards have many tricks to keep themselves alive. Some open a frill of scaly skin around their necks to make them look much bigger. Others have bright blue tongues that they stick out to scare off predators. Lizards are also very good runners and climbers. They have strong legs and rough scales on their feet to help them grip. Some lizards have such hard or spiky scales that if predators do catch them, they are very difficult to eat.

16

◀ A frightened Australian frilled lizard pops out its frill, opens its mouth wide, hisses loudly and thrashes its long tail about.

▼ A male anole lizard stretches out its colorful frill, called a dewlap, to scare off other males.

17

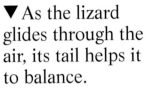

▼ As the lizard glides through the air, its tail helps it to balance.

Flying Lizards

Flying lizards have flaps of scaly skin attached to the sides of their bodies. When they leap into the air, the flaps open out like wings, and the lizards can glide from tree to tree, or to the ground. All flying lizards live in southeastern Asia and the East Indies. Some lizards that do not have these flaps of skin can also jump from trees. They slow their fall by bending their bodies, which act like parachutes.

▶ The flying dragon climbs well but glides to get from one tree to another.

▼ Ribs that stretch out give this lizard bigger "wings."

▲ A flying gecko has webbed feet and a fringed tail to help it glide.

Are these lizards really flying?

19

Living in Trees

Snakes that live in trees have bodies built for climbing and clinging. They are usually very long and thin so they can wind their way through branches. Sometimes they also have a ridge along their bellies for gripping onto twigs and rough bark. A few tree snakes can glide between trees by curving their bellies to make a kind of parachute. Most tree snakes are green or brown to match the rainforests where they live.

Blending in wit

◀ This blunt-headed tree snake is poisonous. It comes out only at night and eats other cold-blooded animals, like lizards.

▲ Green tree pythons are yellow or brown when they hatch. They will turn green by the time they are three years old.

Some snakes can go without food for more than a year.

Scaly Mammals

Mammals are animals that have warm blood and feed their young with milk. Some mammals have scaly tails and others have scaly feet. The only mammal with body scales is the pangolin. Its scales protect it from predators, and from the ants and termites it eats. To keep ants from biting and crawling into its eyes and nostrils when it is feeding, a pangolin has thick lids that cover its eyes and special muscles that close its nostrils. Pangolins have no teeth. Their sticky tongues drag food straight down to their muscular stomachs.

▶ If attacked, a pangolin protects its soft underside by curling into a tight, hard ball.

A pangolin's tongue i

22

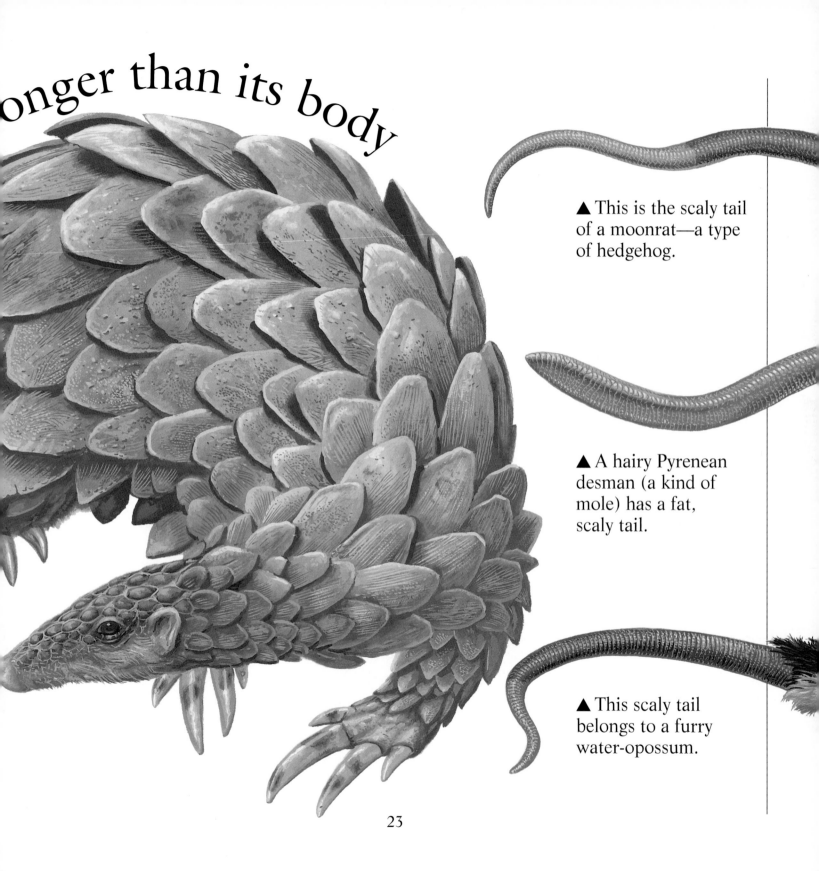

▲ This is the scaly tail of a moonrat—a type of hedgehog.

▲ A hairy Pyrenean desman (a kind of mole) has a fat, scaly tail.

▲ This scaly tail belongs to a furry water-opossum.

23

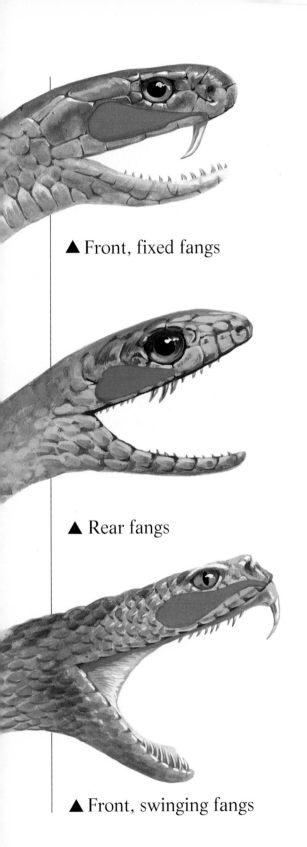

▲ Front, fixed fangs

▲ Rear fangs

▲ Front, swinging fangs

Venomous Snakes

Some snakes squeeze their prey to death. Other snakes kill their prey with poison, known as venom, which comes out of long, hollow teeth called fangs. Venomous snakes have different kinds of fangs and different kinds of venom. Some venom affects the nerves and stops the heart. Some destroys the muscles so the animal cannot run. A few snakes have venom that softens the flesh of the killed animal so it is easier to eat.

◀ Most snakes have fangs in the front of their mouths, but some have fangs at the back. A few have fangs that fold up and swing down.

► A spitting cobra squirts venom to protect itself. Cobras also flatten their necks to look fierce.

◄ A rattlesnake has very long fangs to inject venom deep into its prey.

Some cobras play dead when they are in danger.

Life Underground

Most worm lizards have a blunt tail that looks just like their head.

Worm lizards spend nearly all their time underground. Most of them are legless and tunnel through the ground like worms. They dig with their head, which is toughened with thick scales. The way they dig depends on the shape of their head. Worm lizards have no ears and their eyes are covered with clear skin to protect them from dirt. Unlike worms, they have large, sharp teeth to crush insects.

▶ This spade-headed worm lizard has one big, thick scale on its head. It uses this like a spade to dig through soil.

▶Shovel or spade heads push forward and then up.

▶Chisel heads turn their heads as they push.

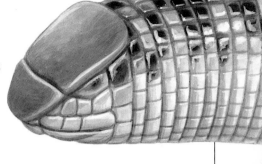

▶Keel heads push forward, then to the side.

▶Round heads push forward and can turn in any direction.

Other titles in the series:

ANIMAL BABIES
INCREDIBLE CREATURES
MIGHTY DINOSAURS
THINGS WITH WINGS
UNDERWATER ANIMALS

Acknowledgments

(t=top, b=bottom, l=left, r=right, c=center, F=front cover, B=back cover)

Simone End, Fb, Ftl, 12/13c, 19tr, 28bl, 32. **Christer Eriksson,** 16/17c, 25tl. **John Francis/Bernard Thornton Artists, UK,** B, 6bl, 24l. **David Kirshner,** 2, 3bl, 4bl, 4/5c, 5tr, 6/7bc, 7tc, 7tr, 8tl, 9bl, 10/11c, 11r, 15bc, 16tl, 17br, 18/19c, 20bl, 25r, 26tl, 26cl, 26bc, 27bc, 27tr, 28/29, 30/31bc, 31t. **Frank Knight,** 20/21c. **James McKinnon,** 1, 22/23c, 23r. **Colin Newman/Bernard Thornton Artists, UK,** 14/15t. **Trevor Ruth,** 3tr, 9tc, 12tl.